AYRSHIRE'S LAST DAYS OF COLLIERY STEAM

Tom Heavyside

After BR had withdrawn the last of its standard gauge steam locomotives in August 1968, many more railway enthusiasts started to take a keen interest in those owned by the NCB, some travelling long distances to witness the action. On the same day as the picture opposite a small group, cameras and tape recording equipment at the ready, gathered at Dunaskin Washery to record the movements of NCB Nos. 19 and 24. On this particular visit the author remembers meeting fellow photographers from as far afield as Birmingham and London.

Text © Tom Heavyside, 2013.
First published in the United Kingdom, 2013,
by Stenlake Publishing Ltd.
Telephone: 01290 551122
www.stenlake.co.uk

ISBN 9781840336207

Further Reading

Tom Heavyside, *Scotland's Last Days of Colliery Steam*, Stenlake Publishing Ltd, 2003.
Guthrie Hutton, *Mining: Ayrshire's Lost Industry*, Stenlake Publishing Ltd, 1996.
David L. Smith, *The Dalmellington Iron Company*, David & Charles, 1967.

Acknowledgements

My sincere thanks are due to the following for their ready help in the completion of this volume: Paul Abell, Peter Barber, David Cross, Bob Darvill, David Dawson, Mrs Morag Dempster, Roger Hateley, Barry Hoper, Eddie Johnson, Bill Roberton, Archie Thom, David Young and the staff of Wigan Heritage Service.

Photographic Credits

Adrian Booth: page 38.
Derek Cross: pages 2, 8, 10, 14–19, 22–23, 26–35, 37, 39–41.
W.A.C. Smith/Transport Treasury: page 9.
Tom Heavyside: front cover, inside front cover and pages 1, 4, 5, 7, 11–13, 20, 21, 24, 25, 42–48, inside back cover, back cover.

Right: On its way back to the Waterside Railway, near Dalmellington, after a brief loan to Auchincruive Colliery (known as Glenburn) at Prestwick, Andrew Barclay works No. 1985, NCB No. 18, built in 1930, crosses the River Ayr at the approach to Ayr Station on 19 March 1965. This was a lengthy seventeen-mile journey for an NCB locomotive. No. 18 was purchased by the NCB in 1955 from the Coltness Iron Company of Newmains, near Wishaw, for the Waterside Railway, where it was most unpopular with the engine crews as it was the only engine with inside cylinders. It was somewhat sarcastically dubbed 'The Coltness Gem'. Few tears were shed the following September when it was scrapped.

Introduction

The early coal workings in Ayrshire were concentrated mainly in the north of the county, from the late seventeenth century much of the output being shipped across the North Channel to Ireland. Later the founding of ironworks at Muirkirk and Glenbuck and the subsequent expansion of this industry during the middle years of the nineteenth century led to a huge increase in demand for the black gold, resulting in the sinking of new pits in central Ayrshire. The simultaneous development of the main railway network enabled the coal owners to access markets that previously were simply out of reach.

While the last of the blast furnaces in Ayrshire was shut down in 1928, coal continued to play an important role in the economy of the county. However during the difficult years leading up to the Second World War, following various amalgamations the surviving pits became owned by just seven companies, with over seventy five per cent of the total output coming from mines managed by the giant combine Bairds & Dalmellington Ltd.

When the coal industry was nationalised on 1 January 1947 the newly-created National Coal Board became responsible for thirty-two collieries in Ayrshire. Among the myriad items of equipment handed over to the new owners were twenty-two steam locomotives (six dating from Victorian times) for local trip and shunting requirements. Usually referred to as 'pugs', twenty had a 0-4-0 wheel arrangement and carried their water supplies in a saddle tank, the other two being 0-6-0 side tanks. Eleven had been built by the Kilmarnock firm of Andrew Barclay Sons & Co. Ltd, the other eleven having originated in the factories of six other private locomotive builders.

In 1947 the NCB provided employment for some 10,160 men in Ayrshire, a total of 3,265,000 tons of coal being brought to the surface that year. Over the next fourteen years the NCB invested much capital in modernising the industry, some of the smaller collieries being closed down while a number of new drift mines were opened. The most ambitious scheme was that commenced in December 1952 with the cutting of the first sod for what was to be the showcase Killoch Colliery at Ochiltree, where eventually it was aimed to employ 3,300 men with a production target of 6,000 tons per day.

In 1960, thirteen years after the state took control of the coal industry, twenty-seven collieries were operating in Ayrshire, and that year they excavated a grand total of 2,690,000 tons of coal with 11,260 men being in the employ of the NCB. It will be noted that productivity was lower than in 1947, more men being employed with less output. However 790 of these men were already based at Killoch where the coal cutters had only just been started up, the new mine contributing a meagre 27,000 tons in 1960. Prior to this many experienced, otherwise redundant miners had been retained pending transfer to Killoch.

Throughout the 1960s steam locomotives continued to have a vital role at some collieries. For example, in March 1967 – when for administrative purposes the Ayrshire mines were incorporated into a new Scottish South Area (by which time British Railways had already dispensed with steam in the area) – eighteen remained in the county. The fleet at that time consisted of fifteen 0-4-0STs and three 0-6-0Ts for use at six locations. Two of the survivors had been built back in the Victorian era, the oldest in 1885, while five were comparative youngsters having been bought by the NCB from Andrew Barclay between 1947 and 1955. Indeed no less than fourteen of the fleet had been fashioned in their Kilmarnock workshops. By 1967 diesel locomotives had also infiltrated the scene, with three allocated to Killoch Colliery, Ochiltree, and one to Barony Colliery, Auchinleck.

Over the ensuing years one by one the Ayrshire collieries fell silent and in consequence the need for locomotives gradually declined. However, regular steam lingered on until Friday, 7 July 1978 when Pennyvenie Colliery at Dalmellington closed and its last coal was transported down the Doon Valley to the washery at Dunaskin. After this a locomotive was steamed very occasionally at Barony Colliery when required to substitute for the regular diesel, with a last reported use in January 1979. Ten years later, in 1989, deep mining in Ayrshire came to an end when Barony itself was closed down.

Today there are very few reminders on the ground of this once vital Ayrshire industry, the most noticeable feature being the distinctive 'A'-frame headgear that still stands on the site of the former Barony Colliery at

Auchinleck. Regarding the steam locomotives once owned by the NCB in the county, nine have been preserved – all built by Andrew Barclay – with four, most appropriately, in the care of the Ayrshire Railway Preservation Group whose headquarters occupy the site of the old Dalmellington Iron Company at Waterside.

On a personal note it was not until August 1973 that I first ventured north from my Lancashire home to Ayrshire in search of NCB steam, by which time it was confined to just four locations. Thus I am much indebted to others who were active in earlier years for many of the photographs in this volume. In particular it has been a privilege to draw on the work of the late Derek Cross, courtesy of his son David. An Ayrshire farmer, Derek Cross was one of the most eminent photographers of the Scottish railway scene in the 1960s, his main line images of both steam and diesel locomotives regularly featuring in contemporary periodicals. He also authored many books on the subject and fortunately did not ignore the local industrial railways.

The compilation of this book has evoked for me many happy memories of days spent amid the Ayrshire countryside, undoubtedly enriched by a number of friendly engine crews. Such days spent observing steam in a working environment, although long gone and impossible to recreate, will never be forgotten.

Left: Fifty-five year old Andrew Barclay 0-4-0ST works No. 1614, NCB No. 19, exerts maximum power working upgrade along the Waterside Railway, shortly after leaving Dunaskin Washery with a set of empties destined for Pennyvenie Colliery on 30 August 1973. The engine was on very familiar territory, having remained at the Waterside Railway ever since being delivered new from the maker's Caledonia Works, Kilmarnock, in 1918.

Today the most prominent reminder of 'Ayrshire's Lost Industry' is the landmark 180ft-high 'A'-frame headgear that continues to overlook the landscape at the site of the 1989-closed Barony Colliery, by the quiet B7036 Auchinleck to Ochiltree road. It can be seen for miles around. Overshadowed by the structure on 20 May 1974 is Andrew Barclay 0-4-0ST works No. 2369, NCB No. 8, built in 1955.

Well-known Waterside driver Tom Bruce carries out the vital task of oiling round the motion of NCB No. 24 on 21 May 1974. His father, Tom Bruce senior, had also been a driver on the railway.

Andrew Barclay Sons & Co. Ltd

As mentioned in the introduction, the collieries in Ayrshire depended heavily on steam locomotives constructed by Andrew Barclay Sons & Co. Ltd, their products totally monopolising the scene during the last years of steam from 1970. But it should also be noted that the influence of this Kilmarnock company extended far beyond the Ayrshire boundary and their engines could be seen not only throughout Britain but in many countries overseas.

The company can trace its history back to 1842 when Andrew Barclay founded a small engineering business in Kilmarnock supplying various products to local mills etc. In 1847 the business moved to the present Caledonia Works, close by Kilmarnock Station, from where he supplied machinery, including winding engines, to the burgeoning coal and iron industries. His first venture into steam locomotive manufacture, a small 0-4-0ST for the Portland Iron Works at Hurlford, left the factory in 1859. Unfortunately some of the early records have been lost, but it is understood that about one hundred locomotives had been finished by 1870 and the firm had expanded to become the largest in Kilmarnock with 420 men on the payroll.

Even so, financially life was far from easy and to help protect the future Barclay provided the necessary capital for a seemingly independent partnership formed by his brother and four sons to carry out similar work in the town from the Riverbank Works by the River Irvine. Trading as Barclays & Co. their first locomotive was completed in August 1872. It is believed to have been allocated works number 201 in line with the practice of some new entrants to the market of starting their numerical lists higher than at No. 1 to give the impression of a well-established business. In total approximately 124 steam engines were built by Barclays & Co. before production as a separate concern officially finished in 1888, when the two works' lists were combined, the next engine leaving the Caledonia Works as No. 636.

Somehow over the years the firm managed to survive a number of financial crises, including an ill-fated venture into iron making at Workington, before the business was incorporated as a limited company in 1892. As Andrew Barclay Sons & Co. Ltd they fostered a growing reputation for the supply of small, sturdy, reliable locomotives, colliery owners being prominent among a varied customer base. From 1893 until the end of the First World War an average of thirty-one locomotives left the Caledonia Works each year, numbers fluctuating from a low of twelve in 1895 to a high of fifty-one in 1917.

Inevitably, due to the parlous state of the economy during the inter-war years production declined, despite the fillip of an order from the London Midland & Scottish Railway for twenty-five of the Fowler-designed '4F' 0-6-0s. These were delivered over thirteen months from January 1927, later running as British Railways Nos. 44357 to 44381. About 1935 the company produced its first diesel shunter, a side of the business that was to prove increasingly important in later years.

During the 1940s the company built 191 steam locomotives, notable among them fifteen 'Austerity' 0-6-0STs to a wartime design developed by the Hunslet Engine Company of Leeds for the Ministry of Supply. The frames for a further ninety-five engines constructed to traditional Barclay patterns were laid in the 1950s, the last departing Kilmarnock in 1956. The erecting shop was then able to give its undivided attention to diesel production, including fifty small shunters for BR during the five years from 1956.

However there was to be a brief steam renaissance in the early 1960s, first in 1961 when the last of 114 fireless locomotives was released. Then the following year a 0-6-2 tender engine was built for an Indonesian client, the order having originally been won by W.G. Bagnall of Stafford but switched to Kilmarnock after they had ceased locomotive building. All told, Andrew Barclay constructed some 2,150 steam locomotives.

While it is now many years since any Andrew Barclay steam locomotives were used commercially, perhaps no finer tribute can be paid to the company than the fact that over 130 have been preserved, the oldest dating from 1891. While widely dispersed around Britain, it is appropriate that a 0-4-0ST, although not one that saw colliery service, is back where it started life in 1940: on display at the Caledonia Works, West Langlands Street, Kilmarnock, now operating under the name Wabtec Rail Scotland.

A typical Andrew Barclay 0-4-0ST, NCB No. 21, at Cairnhill drift mine, Cronberry, on 21 May 1974. The engine was supplied new to the NCB as works No. 2284 in 1949 with 3ft 7in. diameter wheels set to a wheelbase of 6ft 0in., which allowed it to negotiate some quite tight curves. The outside cylinders measured 16in. diameter with a 24in. stroke. Total length over buffers was 24ft 10in. The vertical sided, curved-topped saddle tank could carry up to 1,030 gallons of water and in full working order the engine tipped the scales at 35 tons. Tractive effort calculated at 85% of maximum boiler pressure of 160lb. per square inch was a useful 19,432lb. The Ramsbottom safety valves can be seen protruding above the dome. It is painted black with red and yellow lining, the legend on the saddle tank NCB West Ayr Area belonging to an earlier administrative era, the area not having existed since 1 January 1963 when it merged with East Ayr Area to form a new Ayrshire Area.

Inset: A close-up of the cast Andrew Barclay identification plate measuring 9¾in. x 7¼in. attached to the cab side detailing its works number and year of manufacture. The upper plate signifies the engine was registered with the Railway Executive and permitted by BR to run over designated lines such as the exchange sidings, subject to periodic examination.

Grant Ritchie & Co.

In addition to Andrew Barclay Sons & Co. Ltd and the closely allied Barclays & Co., four other private locomotive manufacturers had workshops in Kilmarnock. Furthermore, the Glasgow & South Western Railway also established its main works in the town. However, after 1967 the only Kilmarnock-built engine to be found on NCB tracks in Ayrshire other than those by Andrew Barclay, was one constructed by Grant Ritchie & Co. in 1911.

The Grant Ritchie partnership was in fact formed by two former Andrew Barclay employees, Thomas Maxwell Grant and William Ritchie, together with local doctor James McAlister, to take over the engineering business of the late George Caldwell housed at the Townholm Works on the north side of Kilmarnock in 1876. Andrew Taylor, a third defector from Andrew Barclay, joined the partnership shortly afterwards.

Grant Ritchie supplied a diverse range of machinery, including more than forty mainly four-coupled steam locomotives, to its various customers. The engines, it must be said, bore a striking resemblance to those designed by Andrew Barclay. The works list made no distinction between locomotives and other manufactured items, and thus the last locomotive to leave the Townholm Works in 1919 was allocated works number 865. The assets of the business were disposed of to the Kilmarnock Foundry Co. Ltd in 1920.

Twenty-seven years later, in 1947, fifteen Grant Ritchie locomotives were itemised on the initial inventory of the NCB Scottish Division, including three domiciled in Ayrshire. Just two (none from Ayrshire) remain in existence, a 0-4-0ST dating from 1894 now at the Ribble Steam Railway at Preston, Lancashire, and a 0-4-2ST built in 1914 at the Prestongrange Mining Museum, Prestonpans, East Lothian.

The last Ayrshire-based Grant Ritchie locomotive to remain in service, works No. 531, NCB No. 23, built in 1911, propels wagons along the Waterside Railway, north of Dunaskin Washery, on 27 May 1963. Its Kilmarnock (Barclay) pedigree is very evident.

Neilson & Co.

During the late 1960s only three locomotives not built in Kilmarnock remained in the Ayrshire coalfield, including two four-coupled saddle tanks from the nineteenth century put together by the Glasgow firm Neilson & Co. In their last days both were allocated to Barony Colliery, Auchinleck.

Neilson's origins go back to about the year 1836, initially manufacturing marine and stationary engines, the guiding light Walter Neilson working with various partners during the early years. Their first locomotives took to the rails of the Garnkirk & Glasgow Railway in 1843 and not long afterwards the firm began to specialise in locomotive construction. The business expanded rapidly and in 1861 the decision was taken to move from their old and by then inadequate premises near Anderston Quay to what later became the world-renowned Hyde Park Works in the Springburn district of the city.

Neilson then entered into partnership with James Reid, the latter becoming sole proprietor when Neilson left after some disagreement during the mid-1870s. Later, in 1884, Neilson founded the Clyde Locomotive Co. Ltd, trading from premises just across the way from the Hyde Park factory. This venture did not last long, the works being occupied from 1888 by Sharp Stewart & Co. who relocated their business from Manchester.

The much-respected James Reid continued to run Neilson's until 1892, the year before he died, when a new partnership agreement was drawn up to include his four sons, the letterheads being amended to the more appropriate Neilson Reid & Co. in 1898. By then it was the largest private locomotive manufacturing company in Britain, employing some 3,000 men.

In 1903 the momentous decision was taken to amalgamate Neilson Reid with its two main Glasgow rivals, Dübs & Co. (established in 1863 by another former Neilson partner) and Sharp Stewart & Co., to form the North British Locomotive Co. Before the merger it is estimated that Neilson's had completed over 5,800 locomotives, a high percentage having been shipped down the Clyde to various countries overseas.

In 1947 the NCB in Scotland became the owners of ten very similar Neilson 0-4-0STs built between 1876 and 1901 (the final one carrying Neilson Reid plates). Unfortunately none of those that worked in Ayrshire have been preserved, but two that had spells based in neighbouring Lanarkshire have survived, one at the Bo'ness & Kinneil Railway, the other at the Chasewater Railway, Brownhills, Staffordshire.

Right: The distinctive profile of a Neilson 0-4-0ST is seen to advantage at Barony Colliery, Auchinleck, on 19 May 1967. At the time it was the most elderly locomotive in Ayrshire, having left the maker's Hyde Park Works in Glasgow as works No. 3452 in 1885. Note the saddle tank does not extend fully over the firebox and smokebox as on the Andrew Barclay and Grant Ritchie locomotives featured in this volume.

During the late 1960s the only engine to be found in Ayrshire that hadn't been built in Scotland was Hawthorn Leslie 0-4-0ST works No. 3351, NCB No. 20, which was despatched from the maker's Forth Banks Works in Newcastle-upon-Tyne to the Dalmellington Iron Company in 1918. It had 14in. x 22in. cylinders and 3ft 6in. diameter wheels. It was based at Mauchline Colliery from 1952 and is seen here on 22 August 1967. The chalked, partly smudged message on the side of the cab – 'This Pug is for Monday' – and the more boldly written 'OFF' (twice), clearly indicates that the engine had already run its last. By the initials on the cab side, presumably it was 'TG' who decreed it was no longer fit to steam. The design features of No. 20 can be compared to those of a standard Andrew Barclay product, NCB No.16, running by in reverse gear. No. 20 was scrapped in May 1969, still sporting the light green livery with white lining (although hardly discernible) as applied by Bairds & Dalmellington prior to Nationalisation in 1947.

Mauchline Colliery was located about one and a half miles north of the small town of that name. Often referred to as Dykefield, the name of the immediate locale, it was sunk in 1925 by Kilmarnock-based Caprington & Auchlochan Collieries Ltd, the owners of three other collieries, but was acquired in 1934 by Bairds & Dalmellington Ltd after the former went into liquidation. Later, under the stewardship of the NCB in 1947, Mauchline recorded an output of 276,000 tons of coal with 770 men employed at the site. While coal ceased to be cut from the seams in 1966 the preparation plant continued for a few more years, washing coal brought in by road from the drift mines at Lochlea and Sorn that had been opened in the early 1950s. With the screens in the background, Andrew Barclay 0-4-0ST works No. 1116, NCB No. 16, bides time in the overgrown yard on 30 August 1973. Like No. 20 (opposite), No. 16 was also originally owned by the Dalmellington Iron Company but had slightly larger 16in. x 24in. cylinders and 3ft 8in. wheels, making it the more powerful of the two. While the works plate attached to No. 16 stated its year of manufacture as 1910, it was actually put together in 1907, being held in stock at the maker's Kilmarnock premises for three years before its sale for use on the Waterside Railway. It first came to Mauchline in 1956.

Opposite: Mauchline, in common with most collieries, possessed facilities for merchants to collect coal for distribution to local households and businesses. Seen here behind No. 16, on the same day as the picture on page 11, is the elevator that fed the hopper with coal ready for bagging. On the left a lorry arrives from Sorn with yet more coal for washing. As well as shunting the yard, the locomotive tripped wagons along the one and a quarter mile branch to the BR exchange sidings at Garrochburn Junction, on the ex-Glasgow & South Western Railway Glasgow to Carlisle main line.

Right: Nestling at the back of the one-road, brick-built engine shed at Mauchline in August 1973, raised on blocks and ostensibly under repair, is Andrew Barclay 0-4-0ST works No. 1442, NCB No. 11. Note the maker's identification plate has been removed from the cab side sheet; while this was dated 1919, it was actually built about three years earlier, being held in stock by Andrew Barclay until eventually purchased by Caprington & Auchlochan Collieries in 1919. The engine then spent nearly forty years at Auchlochan Collieries, near Coalburn, Lanarkshire, before moving to Ayrshire where it had short spells at Barony, Kames, Bank and Killoch collieries before transferring to Mauchline in 1969. The preparation plant was closed down in February 1974, No. 11 being disposed of when the site was cleared early in 1976. No. 16 fared better in that it was reallocated to Barony Colliery in August 1974.

The NCB began preparatory work on sinking the 2,490ft-deep Killoch Colliery at Ochiltree, in a previously untapped area of the coalfield, in December 1952. However it wasn't until December 1960 – and after £7 million had been expended – that any coal was brought to the surface. While a seemingly staggering one million tons was raised in 1965, and at its peak over 2,300 men worked on the site, the pit never lived up to the high expectations originally envisaged, mainly due to some serious geological faulting of the otherwise rich seams. In keeping with its status as a modern pit, both in respect of machinery and working conditions, the NCB intended to use diesel locomotives on the surface railway but on at least four occasions, usually at short notice, steam had to be drafted in from elsewhere to cover. Andrew Barclay 0-4-0ST works No. 1442, NCB No. 11, arrived here in May 1967 from Lugar Central Workshops and stayed until early 1969 when it left for Mauchline. No. 11 was in charge of proceedings on 1 August 1967 when it was photographed running light engine through the yard past the lofty concrete towers which enclosed the electric winding mechanism over the shafts (opposite) and also shunting a rake of wooden-sided wagons (above). The large square-shaped dumb buffers helped prevent buffer locking when travelling round tight curves. Note that the Andrew Barclay works plate was still attached to the cab side at this time (see page 13). The shunter, sporting a rather distinctive patterned jumper, certainly seemed happy to be working with steam. Sadly, after a life lasting a mere twenty-seven years Killoch closed in 1987, the coal preparation plant being retained for processing opencast coal, as was the rail access via the old Glasgow & South Western route from Annbank Junction, near Ayr.

Opposite: William Baird & Company instigated sinking the original two shafts at Barony Colliery, Auchinleck, alongside the road to Ochiltree, in 1906. Completed in 1912 to a depth of 2,046 feet, it was then the deepest mine in Scotland. In 1938, under the Bairds & Dalmellington banner, work started on a third shaft but this was summarily brought to a standstill in 1940 due to wartime constraints. It was eventually finished by the NCB in 1950. A significant development in the area was the opening of Barony Power Station by the South of Scotland Electricity Board in 1957, the generators burning dried colliery slurry obtained from the adjacent Barony Colliery, as well as from other Ayrshire pits. Five years later, in 1962, the colliery experienced serious problems when No. 2 shaft started to break down, as did No. 1 while remedial work was in progress, blocking the ventilation system and leaving the NCB with no alternative but to lay-off over 1,000 men. A new No. 4 shaft enabled production to restart in 1966. After reopening, the revived colliery had the distinction of being the last stamping ground of a pair of vintage Neilson 0-4-0STs. Seen here coupled to a well-laden internal user wagon in September 1966, shortly after its arrival at Barony from Lugar Central Workshops, is works No. 3452, NCB No. 2, which was built in 1885 at Neilson's Hyde Park Works, Glasgow. By this time it was the oldest locomotive in Ayrshire.

Below: In October the following year the sprightly octogenarian finds its way towards the exchange sidings blocked by a brake van and BR Class 08 diesel-electric No. D3529 (later renumbered 08414). There was an age difference of seventy-three years between the two locomotives, the latter having been released from Derby Works in June 1958. In the background, on the far right of the picture, a BR Class 20 locomotive can be seen hauling yet more coal wagons south along the Kilmarnock to Dumfries line.

In early April 1968 No. 2 suffered a broken spring at Barony and fellow Neilson 0-4-0ST works No. 4775, NCB No. 4, built in 1894, was hastily despatched from Lugar Central Workshops to cover. Later that same month, against a backcloth of colliery buildings and the power station cooling towers, a vibrant No. 4 runs past the laid-low No. 2. On the footplate of the former a young David Cross enjoys the experience courtesy of the driver, while his father busies himself with a camera, illustrative of the friendliness of the NCB engine crews referred to in the introduction. While both engines were built to the same specifications with 14in. x 20in. outside cylinders and 3ft 8in. wheels, a close examination of the two engines reveals some detail differences, particularly the cab profiles, evidence of No. 4's rebuilding by Andrew Barclay in 1929. No. 4 was also fitted with dumb buffers. Both locomotives were painted green with red rods, No. 4 looking quite resplendent, not yet having had time to become work-stained like its older sister. Boldly stencilled on the saddle tank of No. 4 is the legend 'Scottish South Area' (formed in March 1967), the author knowing of no other locomotive so identified.

Somewhat ironically, the month after No. 4 had made its debut at Barony it was followed from Lugar by the youngest steam locomotive on the books of the NCB in Ayrshire, Andrew Barclay 0-4-0ST works No. 2369, NCB No. 8. Completed in 1955 with 16in. x 24in. cylinders and 3ft 7in. wheels, No. 8 initially worked at Bank Colliery, New Cumnock. No less than seventy years the junior of the elder statesman at Barony, Neilson NCB No. 2, the youngster demonstrates its prowess as it draws three wooden-sided and four steel-bodied wagons away from the screens in April 1969. Over forty wagons are evident in the picture. Behind the screens can be seen the 'A'-frame supports for the two pairs of winding wheels set at different levels.

Below: A few minutes later, with the blast from the exhaust ringing out loud and clear, No. 16 continues its battle against the gradient as it slowly makes its way towards the exchange sidings. In autumn 1982, after having been away for twenty-six years, No. 16 returned to its old haunts on the Waterside Railway courtesy of the Ayrshire Railway Preservation Group (see inside back cover). Now a centenarian, it can still be seen at the Scottish Industrial Railway Centre at Dunaskin, near Dalmellington.

Above: In mid-August 1974 Andrew Barclay 0-4-0ST works No. 1116, NCB No. 16, was moved from Mauchline Coal Preparation Plant the few miles south to Barony. Having first taken to the rails of the Waterside Railway, near Dalmellington, back in 1910, following the disposal for scrap of the two Neilson 0-4-0STs at Barony (No. 4 in 1969 and No. 2 in 1970) No. 16 became senior servant among the remaining locomotives in Ayrshire. Seen here on 26 August 1974, a few days after arriving at Barony, the veteran struggles for adhesion as it hauls some BR 44-ton capacity 'merry-go-round' wagons away from the colliery yard.

Three months earlier, on 20 May 1974, No. 8 was found resting in the colliery yard at Barony. It also left for pastures new in 1982 but in far away Yorkshire where it now resides on the Derwent Valley Light Railway at Murton, near York. Surprisingly, that same year another Andrew Barclay 0-4-0ST, works No. 2296, NCB No. 17, built in 1950, was transported to Barony from Bedlay Colliery, Glenboig, three miles north of Coatbridge, to be the spare loco to the resident diesels. It is understood it was never called upon at Barony and in September 1989 became the very last steam locomotive to be disposed of by British Coal, as the state-owned coal industry was then styled prior to privatisation. It is currently based at the Scottish Vintage Bus Museum at Lathalmond, near Dunfermline, Fife. Prior to closure in 1989, Barony had the distinction of being the last operational deep mine in Ayrshire, the adjacent power station having stopped generating six years earlier in 1983. Subsequently when the colliery shafts were capped and the site cleared, the huge welded steel 'A' frame, complete with its four winding wheels, was left standing as a monument to the valued role coal had played in the economic and social development of the county. In contrast to its former days the immediate area around the frame now provides a pleasant picnic site. Nearby a small memorial stone inscribed 'Erected in Memory of Those Who Worked and Lost Their Lives in the Barony Colliery 1908–1989' serves as a poignant reminder of the high cost paid by some in winning the coal.

Lugar Central Workshops, just east of Cumnock, were established about 1954 on the site of the recently closed Lugar mine. The repair and maintenance of locomotives was part of its remit, and sadly on occasions the dismantling of worn out engines that were uneconomic to repair. When photographed on 2 August 1967 Andrew Barclay 0-4-0ST works No. 1345, NCB No. 7, built in 1913, was surrounded by a host of miscellaneous items of dumped machinery, the end coming a few weeks later. Its home for the first thirty-eight years of its life was the Waterside Railway, near Dalmellington, prior to a transfer to Bank Colliery, New Cumnock, in 1951, followed by a move to Barony Colliery, Auchinleck, six years later. Locomotive repair work ceased at Lugar in 1968.

Left: With the shunter riding on the footplate steps, green-liveried Andrew Barclay 0-4-0ST works No. 2368, NCB No. 1, built in 1955, leads eight wagons down the incline from Cairnhill drift mine, Cronberry, towards the BR Gasswater exchange sidings in April 1968. The train has just passed under the A70 Edinburgh to Ayr road. This one-mile, steeply graded branch originally linked the Anglo-Austral Mines Ltd Gasswater Barytes (barium sulphate) Mine with the ex-Glasgow & South Western Railway Ayr to Muirkirk line. The Cairnhill drift was close to the barytes mine and when opened in 1954 the NCB came to an agreement with Anglo-Austral that they would also handle their coal traffic. However in 1960, following the demise of the Anglo-Austral locomotive in the autumn of the previous year, roles were reversed, the NCB then taking over the branch and becoming responsible for the flow of wagons to and from both mines. The barytes mine closed in 1964.

Right: The crew of BR diesel-electric Bo-Bo Class 20 No. 8027 (later renumbered 20027), look on as No. 1 rumbles into the Gasswater sidings by the old Cronberry Station, with coal from Cairnhill on 24 November 1971. No. 8027 was only four years younger than No. 1, having emerged from English Electric's former Robert Stephenson & Hawthorns works at Darlington in December 1959. It continued to be maintained by BR for a further eleven years before being withdrawn at the end of 1982. By 1971 the only means of access to the Gasswater sidings was from Auchinleck Junction, just north of Cumnock on the main Kilmarnock to Dumfries line, the other routes from the west having already been closed, as had the section further east towards Muirkirk. The passenger service through Cronberry had ended back in September 1951.

Here No. 1 more or less obstructs the entrance to the brick-built engine shed at Cairnhill on 21 May 1974. Erected in 1960 to protect the engines at this bleak outpost, only the left-hand door still hangs in position, presumably its counterpart having had to be removed sometime in the past. No. 1 first came to Cairnhill from Barony Colliery towards the end of 1959 when the Anglo-Austral engine failed, later leaving for Bank Colliery at New Cumnock in 1961 before returning in 1965. Today No. 1 remains in its native Ayrshire at the Scottish Industrial Railway Centre at Dunaskin.

Opposite: Another view from 21 May 1974. The loading hoppers at Cairnhill are on the left while the entrance to the drift is hidden on the right, as Andrew Barclay 0-4-0ST works No. 2284, NCB No. 21, built in 1949, awaits its next duty. The engine had been relocated here from the Waterside Railway the previous autumn. In the foreground is the start of the line down to the Gasswater sidings. One of a number of drift mines opened in the area during the early 1950s, Cairnhill produced a total of 23,000 tons of coal for industrial purposes in 1955, its first full year of production when seventy-one men were listed on the payroll. By 1962 the number of men clocking on here had increased to 223 and that year 77,341 tons were loaded onto the conveyor that carried the coal along the tunnel from below ground to the surface. Activity at Cairnhill came to an end in 1977, movements by rail being rather spasmodic in its last years. Happily No. 21 now resides in a secure environment at the Scottish Mining Museum, based at the former Lady Victoria Colliery, Newtongrange, Midlothian.

Industry first came to Muirkirk on the eastern fringes of Ayrshire when a tar works was opened in 1786, followed shortly afterwards by an ironworks that completely transformed the former village. Later, in 1856, the ironworks and a number of small mines sunk in the vicinity became part of the William Baird & Company empire. Kames Colliery, under Baird's control from its inception in 1870, became the major source of employment in the town after the blast furnaces at the ironworks were blown out in 1923. In 1947 some 575 men signed-on daily at Kames (1,000 had once been employed at the ironworks), the pit yielding 149,000 tons of coal for gas and industrial purposes that year. At the start of the 1960s, 555 men worked at the pit when output totalled 124,000 tons per annum. Here Andrew Barclay 0-4-0ST works No. 1653, NCB No. 12, built in 1920 and recently arrived from Lugar Central Workshops, shunts some BR standard 16-ton capacity wagons in September 1966. The engine had 14in x 22in. cylinders and 3ft 5in. wheels.

No. 12, seen again at Kames on 22 August 1967, with some NCB internal user wooden sided wagons in the colliery yard. The one road, brick built engine shed on the right had been in use since 1960, the engines previously being housed on the old ironworks site near Muirkirk Station. Note the enormous pile of waste material (or 'bing' as this was known in Scotland) dominating the background and on the left one of the lofty concrete towers hiding the electric winding gear above the shafts. No. 12 spent the early part of its career in Staffordshire at Gibbons (Dudley) Ltd Dibdale Fireclay Works, where it became redundant in the late 1930s. It then lay dormant for some time before being sold to local scrap-dealers Cashmores of Great Bridge, eventually being acquired by the NCB via Andrew Barclay in 1947. However, after having to be taken out of service in December 1967 there was to be no second reprieve, and it was scrapped at Lugar Central Workshops in November 1968.

When No. 12 suddenly succumbed at Kames towards the end of 1967 arrangements were quickly made to transfer Grant Ritchie 0-4-0ST works No. 531, NCB No. 23, built in 1911, from the Waterside Railway (see page 37). The engine set out from its former home on Saturday 9 December on what proved a most eventful journey. First it was delayed by a hot axlebox at Ayr, and then, with the one-time plentiful water columns in the area having all been decommissioned following the end of BR steam, it had difficulty finding sufficient water, resulting in the engine blowing a fusible plug near Auchinleck. After being abandoned for the night it was rescued the next day by BR Class 25 diesel-electric No. D7618 (later No. 25268) and propelled down the branch to Muirkirk, where after some hasty repairs it was ready for work on the Monday morning. Seen here four months later on a wintry day in April 1968, No. 23 shunts some loaded wagons in the BR exchange sidings by the closed Muirkirk Station. The wagons would later depart along the former Glasgow & South Western Railway line towards Auchinleck.

On the same day as the previous picture No. 23 is seen coupled to BR standard 16-ton capacity mineral wagon No. B550592, built by the Birmingham Railway Carriage & Wagon Company in 1957. Literally thousands of such wagons were supplied to BR by a number of manufacturers. Three months later, on 12 July 1968, the miners at Kames collected their pay packets for the very last time, No. 23 subsequently finding a new home at Cairnhill before moving to Killoch Colliery, Ochiltree. It was scrapped at Killoch during autumn 1971. Still fresh in the minds of Muirkirk residents at the time the pit closed was an underground explosion in November 1957 when seventeen men lost their lives, the worst mining disaster in Ayrshire. A suitable memorial near the centre of the town provides a permanent reminder of this tragic event.

Prior to nationalisation, Bank Colliery at New Cumnock, where production had started by 1868, and neighbouring Knockshinnoch Castle Colliery, which opened for business in 1942, were owned by New Cumnock Collieries Ltd. During 1947, 121,000 tons of coal was hoisted up the shafts at Bank and 252,000 tons at Knockshinnoch, the collieries employing 285 and 530 men respectively. In 1960 output at Bank had reduced to 59,000 tons (269 men) and at Knockshinnoch to 157,000 tons (681 men). A one-mile long railway connected the two collieries and Andrew Barclay 0-4-0ST works No. 1821, NCB No. 15, built in 1924 with 14in. x 22in. cylinders and 3ft 5in. wheels, was given responsibility for the movements at both sites from 1966. While the last coal was wound at Knockshinnoch in February 1968, the coal preparation plant was retained to wash coal from Bank and other nearby collieries. Seen here on 26 April 1968, No. 15 runs along the BR exchange sidings at Knockshinnoch as a BR English Electric Bo-Bo Class 20 starts its journey back along the one mile branch to Bank Junction, just west of New Cumnock Station, where it would join the Kilmarnock to Dumfries line. On the far right of the picture are the level crossing gates and the crossing keeper's hut by the B741 New Cumnock to Dalmellington road.

Mixed with the coal brought from below ground at both Bank and Knockshinnoch collieries was a prodigious amount of waste deposits (bing). After separation the unwanted material was transported to the tipping site in 15 ton-capacity wagons built by Robert Hudson Ltd of Leeds. Patented in 1875, these widely used wagons were able to self-discharge their contents to either side and then self-upright by means of three pivot points, the wagons normally resting on the central pivot in the upright position. Seen here on the same day as the previous picture, No. 15 reverses four empty Hudson wagons towards the loading hopper at Knockshinnoch. In the background is a vast mound of bing from earlier excavations.

Four months later on a sunlit 9 August 1968, No. 15 shunts the yard at Bank Colliery (opposite), while later the same day (above) it hauls ten empty Hudson wagons away from the tipping grounds. By this time there was little life left in Bank and in May 1969 the colliery produced its last coal, No. 15 meeting its end when broken up on site by Motherwell Machinery & Scrap Co. Ltd in August 1969. Sadly Knockshinnoch Castle Colliery will always be remembered for the tragic events of 7 September 1950 when the workings were suddenly inundated by a basin of liquid peat, killing thirteen men. A further 116 miners were trapped underground for over 40 hours before they were rescued by way of some abandoned Bank passageways. Appropriately the Mineworkers Monument stands on the main street of New Cumnock as a memorial to those who lost their lives in the pursuit of coal, while the Knockshinnoch Commemorative Cairns mark the spot in open countryside above where the happening took place. After the closure of Bank empty coal trains continued to turn off the main line at Bank Junction, Knockshinnoch being used by Scottish Coal for the loading of opencast coal until the site was abandoned in 2006. Similar workings now travel from Bank Junction for about three miles along a re-laid former mineral line to a loading pad at Greenburn.

Fauldhead Colliery at Kirkconnel in the Nith Valley, opened by James Irvine McConnel in 1896, was about four miles beyond the Ayrshire boundary in Dumfriesshire. It is included here as in NCB days the few pits in the latter county were always grouped for management purposes with those in Ayrshire. In fact in 1947 the NCB only acquired three collieries in Dumfriesshire: Fauldhead (output 310,000 tons), the much smaller Gateside (58,000 tons), and Tower (70,000 tons) at Sanquhar, with 1,300 men being employed across the three sites. At the end of 1946 the previous owners, Bairds & Dalmellington Ltd, had three 0-4-0STs based in the county, and these duly became state owned assets. In line with its early policy the NCB opened two small drift mines near Kirkconnel, Rig in 1949 and Roger in 1953, neither site being rail connected. Thus following the abandonment of the Gateside/Tower complex in March 1964 only Fauldhead had need of a locomotive. Seen here during April 1968, Andrew Barclay 0-4-0ST works No. 1382, NCB No. 3, manoeuvres a few empty wagons around the yard. Note the six narrow yellow warning stripes on the buffer beam. When new in 1914 the engine travelled north to Aberdeen Gas Works but four years later was back in the county of its birth, transferred at the behest of the wartime Director of Railway Materials to William Baird's Lugar Ironworks. At an unknown date (certainly before nationalisation) it moved to Muirkirk where it stayed until 1960, thereafter spending further time at Lugar before coming to Fauldhead in October 1963.

On the same day as the photograph opposite, No. 3 clatters over the weighbridge with a couple of loaded wagons ready for collection by BR. The platforms of Kirkconnel Station can be seen on the right, Glasgow Central to Carlisle via Kilmarnock trains still stopping here today. The last coal was brought to the surface at Fauldhead in July 1968, and with Rig mine having ceased production in May 1966, this left only Roger mine in Dumfriesshire, the latter not closing until 1980. No. 3 was scrapped in August 1969.

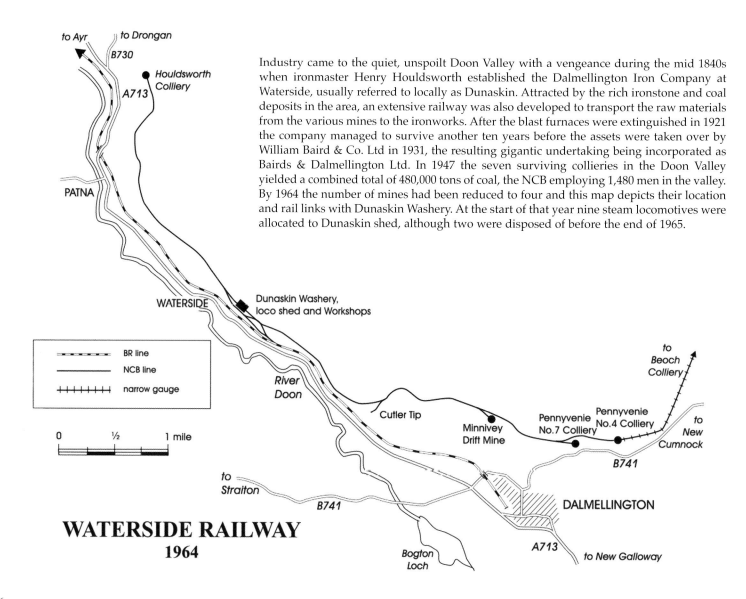

Industry came to the quiet, unspoilt Doon Valley with a vengeance during the mid 1840s when ironmaster Henry Houldsworth established the Dalmellington Iron Company at Waterside, usually referred to locally as Dunaskin. Attracted by the rich ironstone and coal deposits in the area, an extensive railway was also developed to transport the raw materials from the various mines to the ironworks. After the blast furnaces were extinguished in 1921 the company managed to survive another ten years before the assets were taken over by William Baird & Co. Ltd in 1931, the resulting gigantic undertaking being incorporated as Bairds & Dalmellington Ltd. In 1947 the seven surviving collieries in the Doon Valley yielded a combined total of 480,000 tons of coal, the NCB employing 1,480 men in the valley. By 1964 the number of mines had been reduced to four and this map depicts their location and rail links with Dunaskin Washery. At the start of that year nine steam locomotives were allocated to Dunaskin shed, although two were disposed of before the end of 1965.

to Ayr
to Drongan
B730
Houldsworth Colliery
A713
PATNA
WATERSIDE
Dunaskin Washery, loco shed and Workshops

BR line
NCB line
narrow gauge

0   ½   1 mile

River Doon

Cutler Tip

Minnivey Drift Mine

Pennyvenie No.7 Colliery
Pennyvenie No.4 Colliery

to Beoch Colliery

to New Cumnock

B741

to Straiton

B741

DALMELLINGTON

Bogton Loch

A713

to New Galloway

WATERSIDE RAILWAY
1964

Dunaskin Washery, built by the NCB on the old ironworks site three miles north-west of Dalmellington, was effectively the hub of the Waterside Railway. After processing, most of the coal was hauled down to Ayr by way of the BR Dalmellington branch. Pictured on 30 April 1964 Grant Ritchie 0-4-0ST works No. 531, NCB No. 23, built in 1911, is viewed from the footplate of visiting Stanier 'Black 5' 4-6-0 No. 45486, constructed by the London Midland & Scottish Railway at Derby Works in 1943. No. 23 with its 3ft 8in. wheels and 14in. x 22in. cylinders is positively dwarfed by the 63ft 7¾in. long (including tender) and 12ft 10½in. tall (to top of dome) bulk of No. 45486, its driving wheels measuring 6ft 0in., the cylinders 18½in. x 28in. This particular 'Black 5' was a familiar engine around Ayrshire in the early 1960s, being on the books of Ayr shed (coded 67C) from November 1960 until it was withdrawn at the end of 1965 after only twenty-two years service. Meanwhile No. 23, some thirty-two years its senior, soldiered on for a few more years before it was dismantled in October 1971. Nearer the screens, just beyond the weighbridge is an Andrew Barclay 0-6-0T.

On a sunny 26 May 1975 these two Waterside railwaymen appear quite content with their lot as they enjoy a moment of respite on the footplate of Andrew Barclay 0-6-0T works No. 1338, NCB No.17, purchased for the railway in 1913. Note the large cast Andrew Barclay maker's plate, measuring 16¾in. x 11¾in., confirming the engine's pedigree, and the lower Railway Executive registration plate attached in 1952.

Opposite: Houldsworth Colliery, near Patna, named in honour of the founding father of the Dalmellington Iron Company, was at the northern extremity of the Waterside Railway. Coal was first brought to the surface at Houldsworth in 1899, the annual returns for 1947 recording an output of 78,000 tons, when 200 men worked underground supported by another forty on the surface. The 1962 figures were not too dissimilar, 68,118 tons raised by a total workforce of 224. Here No. 17, the first six-coupled engine to grace the Waterside Railway, is seen at Houldsworth on 20 March 1965 in charge of a Branch Line Society special, whose members toured the railway in a couple of brake vans borrowed from BR. No. 17 had 18in. x 24in. cylinders powering 3ft 9in. wheels set to a wheelbase of 6ft 0in. + 5ft 6in. Total length over buffers was 28ft 2¾in. In full working order, with the bunker filled to its 35cwt. capacity and the side tanks 900 gallons of water, it weighed 45 tons. The Ramsbottom safety valves were set to release excess steam when boiler pressure reached 160lb. per square inch, providing a nominal tractive effort of 23,500lb. An early modification was the removal of the flanges from the centre wheels in 1919 following a tragic accident on a reverse curve the previous September. Houldsworth Colliery closed in December 1965, spelling the end for the northernmost section of the railway.

The tour seen overleaf at Houldsworth had earlier departed from Dunaskin heading towards Pennyvenie No. 4 Colliery, the opportunity being taken to propel an empty seven-plank wagon down the line. The cut-down tender wagon with the front removed for ease of shovelling carried additional coal supplies for the locomotive, a standard practice on the Waterside Railway. On the left a Western SMT Leyland PD2 double-decker paces the special along the A713 road with an Ayr–Dalmellington service, while between the highway and the NCB railway is the abandoned trackbed of the former BR Dalmellington branch. This had closed to goods beyond Dunaskin in July 1964, passenger services having been withdrawn the previous April. Above the rear brake van can be seen the meandering waters of the River Doon which flow into the Firth of Clyde just south of Ayr. In the middle distance the obsolete chimneys of the former brickworks jut skywards, while on the right of the photograph another engine is busy near Dunaskin Washery.

A couple of Andrew Barclay engines, 0-6-0T works No. 1785, NCB No. 22, and 0-4-0ST works No. 2284, NCB No. 21, built in 1923 and 1949 respectively, combine forces to push a rake of empty wooden wagons towards the back of Pennyvenie No. 4 Colliery, near Dalmellington, in May 1966. The colliery had actually ceased winding five years earlier in March 1961, the surface buildings being retained to handle coal lifted at Beoch Colliery, which was brought across the moor by way of a narrow gauge railway. When Beoch closed in April 1968 it also meant the end for the short section of line beyond Pennyvenie No. 7 Colliery. Back in 1947, 305 men had been employed at Beoch and 210 at Pennyvenie No. 4, with 101,000 tons and 70,000 tons of household, gas and industrial coal being hauled up the respective shafts. The main design features of No. 22 were similar to those of No. 17 (see page 38) but it had larger side tanks able to hold up to 1,185 gallons of water and it was 18in. longer at 29ft 8¾in., as well as being two tons heavier in full working order at 47 tons. The original chimney had recently been replaced by a shorter version, slightly marring its appearance. No. 22 was scrapped in August 1969 while No. 21 was moved to Cairnhill at the end of 1973 (see pages 7 and 24).

An imposing view of NCB No. 24 as it slowly edges forward under the screens at Pennyvenie No. 7 Colliery on 21 May 1974. This Andrew Barclay 0-6-0T, works No. 2335, was bought new by the NCB for the Waterside Railway in 1953, initially running as West Ayr Area No. 8. However the amalgamation of West and East Ayr areas in January 1963 meant for a time there were two No. 8s operating in the new Ayrshire Area, hence its subsequent renumbering to the more familiar 24. While the cylinders were the same size as those fitted to its much older sisters Nos. 17 and 22 (see page 38), No. 24 had slightly larger 3ft 10in. wheels, but with the boiler able to withstand an increased pressure of 180lb. per square inch was theoretically a little more powerful, having a nominal tractive effort of 25,860lb. However in its early years No. 24 was always regarded as a poor steamer and thus rather unpopular with the engine crews, who much preferred having one of the 0-4-0STs, a problem not solved until February 1965 when a Giesl ejector was fitted. This equipment had been developed by Austrian inventor Dr Adolph Giesl-Gieslingen, the conventional blastpipe and chimney arrangement being replaced by a narrow inward tapering oblong ejector, the exhaust escaping through seven narrow nozzles near the base. In principle this improved the draughting and reduced the amount of fuel burned as well as providing a cleaner exhaust. In total the NCB purchased over forty sets of the equipment, but No. 24 was the only engine in Ayrshire so adapted. The distinctive ejector above the smokebox is seen to advantage in the photograph. The engine was also fitted with a mechanical lubricator and this can be seen fixed to the running plate above the buffer on the left, an unusual feature on an industrial locomotive. A toolbox occupies a similar position on the opposite side.

Opposite: A few minutes later No. 24 shunts seven Hudson side-tipping wagons at Pennyvenie No. 7 Colliery prior to tripping them to Cutler tip. Obviously when the NCB amended the number from 8 to 24 in 1964 only the minimum amount of paint was used, the West Ayr Area lettering being left in situ even though it had been superseded by the new Ayrshire Area. Attached to the well-filled bunker is six-plank tender wagon No. EWA9. In 1947 118,000 tons of coal was brought to the surface here, the efforts of 315 men working below ground and another seventy on the surface. By 1962 production had increased to 221,562 tons, 623 men then descending the shafts to their place of work with a further ninety-five staying above ground. The last coal was drawn in July 1978. After this No. 24 was moved away from Ayrshire to the Bo'ness & Kinneil Railway.

Right: The fireman takes the opportunity for a smoke as Andrew Barclay 0-4-0ST works No. 2244, NCB No. 10, one of the first engines purchased new by the NCB in 1947, blackens the atmosphere at Minnivey drift mine after returning from the tip at Cutler on 26 August 1974. It is attached to tender wagon No. EWA4, clearly marked 'For Internal Use'. The engine was originally identified by the NCB as No. 1, but in 1963 when the West and East Ayr areas were combined, due to a numeric clash with the No. 1 previously domiciled in the old East Ayr Area (see pages 23 and 24), it became No. 10. However, unlike No. 24 (overleaf), the opportunity was taken to apply the correct Ayrshire Area lettering. The first coal was drawn from the steeply inclined drift at Minnivey in 1958, and by the early 1960s it was producing approximately 120,000 tons per annum with some 460 men collecting their weekly pay packets from the office. After a life of only seventeen years the last tubs were dragged from the tunnel in November 1975.

Left: After the NCB ceased using the Waterside Railway in 1978 the Ayrshire Railway Preservation Group established a presence at Minnivey, and among the stock acquired were four former Waterside locomotives, including No. 10. Steam-hauled brake van rides were an attraction for visitors from 1986, as on Sunday 27 July when No. 10, looking a little smarter than in 1974, was observed cautiously threading its way along the overgrown track. In more recent times the group has concentrated its resources down the line at Dunaskin (see inside back cover).

Andrew Barclay 0-4-0ST works No. 1614, NCB No. 19, enters the cutting about half a mile beyond Minnivey on its three mile journey from Pennyvenie to Dunaskin Washery on 30 August 1973. The train had just restarted after pausing at the summit while the shunter pinned-down the wagon brakes in preparation for the descent towards the washery. No. 19 was very familiar with the Waterside Railway, having been bought by the Dalmellington Iron Company from Andrew Barclay in October 1918. It had 16in. x 24in. cylinders and 3ft 8in. wheels, but at 22ft 2¾in. long was slightly shorter than some of the later 'Barclay' products. The engine registered 33 tons on the scales in working order, the saddle tank holding 850 gallons of water. Originally the engine had an open back cab, but much to the relief of the engine crews, especially on days such as this with a strong north-easterly blowing off the moors coupled with intermittent heavy downpours, this was enclosed in about 1922.

In winning the coal from the pits in the Doon Valley a vast amount of waste material was also brought to the surface, which in later years was deposited on the tip at Cutler. Here on 29 August 1973 No. 19 waits impatiently as the last of nine wagons of bing carted from Pennyvenie is tipped. Most unusually the engine is running without a tender wagon. Now over ninety years of age the engine is still at Dunaskin, a valued item on the stock list of the Ayrshire Railway Preservation Group.

Back at Dunaskin Washery the next year on 27 May 1974, No. 10 summons all its reserves in order to push a set of wooden wagons towards the back of the plant. The exchange sidings where BR locomotives collected loaded wagons to be taken down the truncated Dalmellington branch is off the picture to the right.

Viewed from the same standpoint as the picture overleaf, No. 17 comes to the aid of No. 10 in reversing a similar rake of loaded wagons on 26 August 1974. In the foreground, parked on a convenient piece of wasteland by the A713 road, are a Morris Oxford Traveller and two Volkswagen Beetles: the car nearest the camera was the author's mode of transport at the time. Hidden by the overgrown embankment are the tracks leading down to Ayr from the exchange sidings, rails that remain in situ as part of Network Rail, along with a section of the Waterside Railway, for use by coal trains serving the opencast Chalmerston Disposal Point, near the former Minnivey mine. Pleasingly, like its companion (see page 44) No. 17 also lives on, although now resident south of the Border on the Tanfield Railway at Marley Hill, near Gateshead, County Durham.